“In Between The Inspiration”

E. GENE GIVENS

Printed in the United States of America

ISBN:
Softcover: 978-1-969367-87-8
Hardback: 978-1-969367-88-5
eBook: 978-1-969367-86-1

Independently republished by E. Gene Givens.

To order additional copies of this book, contact:

E. Gene Givens
3814 Swift Run Drive
Abingdon, MD 21009-3029

“In Between The Inspiration”

E. GENE GIVENS

DEDICATION

This book is dedicated to my friend and mentor, Jerome Manigan.

For over 45 years, Jerome has always been a source of inspiration to me. I have treasured the creative experiences we shared at Xavier University (1979 to 1981, and beyond. I appreciate that he willingly shared his time, ideas, and advice with me. Unknowingly, he has provided me with many insights, motivations, and inspirations that have driven me to continue to write and publish my work. When we first met, I had written approximately fifty poems, and a couple of short stories. I am sure that i would not have written, or published, over six hundred poems, which has resulted in seven previously published volumes of poetry, and the inspiration and encouragement to write a novel based on my experiences. I am blessed to have known him, and I thank him for his inspiration and friendship.

IN BETWEEN THE INSPIRATION

POETRY

like music
poetry can make you feel
it makes you smile
it makes you laugh, feel sad
or cry, like the tears
from a pealed onion
poetry can take you
anywhere and everywhere
to a memory, a place, or a time . . .
a time when life was so simple
it can take you to a person
a conversation
or an emotion
poetry can lift the human spirit
it can give one hope
where there was none
it can increase cultural awareness
whether contemporary, or historical
poetry can open new ways
and new paths
to express ourselves
in a way that cannot be done
with everyday words
poetry can teach us
the art of creative expression
it can give people an improved ability
to understand one another
poetry can give you power
the power to understand . . .
to understand others
as well as yourself

Pollination

when a poet
poets
to another
poet
many poems
pass through the garden
of imagination
dropping pollen
like bees in flowers . . .
thoughts
words
phases
giving life
to new poems

WE ARE . . .

we are . . .
the beholder of ideas
the witnesses of legends

we are . . .
the tellers of dreams
when we commune with nature
we become sapient tellers
of the unknown

we are . . .
the gate keepers
of the unverifiable myth . . .
enchanted travelers all

we are . . .
the winged carriers of truth
we handle and see
what others only dream of

we are . . .
the bards of old
we live to challenge
the old and the new

we are . . .
the voices of the
unbreakable silence

we are . . . we see . . . we become . . .
and we handle
what others only dream of

we are the sayers
we are the black poets
of yesterday . . . today . . .
and tomorrow

A POET'S DREAM

i wanted to write a poem
that feels
as good as epsom salt
in a hot foot soak
a poem that you could spread just
like a body lotion
and massage
it all over
a poem that could
make you smell the aroma
of hot, hand-made biscuits
on a Sunday morning
or freshly cut grass
on a summer's eve
or freshly popped corn
at a Saturday matinee
a poem that could make you smell
and taste
carnival cotton candy being made
the kind that makes you melt into
a distant daydream
a poem that you want to recite to
your friends
every chance you get
a poem
that will make you pause . . .
and think about it all day
a poem that brings a smile
to every face
and a tear to every eye
. . . alas
tis but a poet's dream

"One Poet's Dream," published in "the Harford Poet," #5, Spring 1992,
The Harford Poetry Society, Forest Hills, MD

IN BETWEEN THE INSPIRATION

he calls himself a
"natural poet"
because little inspires him
but when it happens –
"inspiration"
the words flow without effort
without thought
without correction
i call myself
a poet
because i must work at it . . .
in between the inspiration

"In Between The Inspiration," published in "Shooting Star,"
December 1991, Poetry Press, Pittsburg, TX.

INFATUATED SMILE

"write a poem about me"
she said
with an infatuated smile
on her face
and i thought . . .
how can i write a poem
about you
for you
to you
when you provoke
no image
no emotion no
feeling . . .
i can write blank words
that will pacify your ego
but never your heart
i can write hollow characterizations
but they will never fill the void
  (only time and space)
i can write word that will
describe
but others will know
it's not a poem
but only words
for an infatuated smile

ADMIRATION

please don't tell me
that you admire me
eventually
you will want to come closer
and before long
you will
question your
admiration and
proceed to
dis/mantle/member me
until you have
crushed my heart
and annihilated my being
and soon
you will have forgotten
what it was that you
admired in the first place
leaving me with
scattered pieces
of myself
that i must find
and piece
together for my
next admirer

HAIKU #1: POEM XVIII

we possess great love
but we refuse to share it
and end up alone

Haiku #2: CONFESSIONS

true confessions are
good for the soul but bad for
your reputation

HAIKU #3: YOUR LOVE

it was just enough
to fill my cup, not too much
but enough for me

Haiku #4: SOFT SHOE

people are tapping
to somebody's tune, he to
hers, and me to yours

FAVOR

unlike others
who seeks your favor
i am just a poet
who gives you
words of love
for you to savor

SECRETS

you cannot tell
everyone your
secrets if they
were too hot
for you to keep
then they will
be too hot for
someone to
hold

MEASUREMENTS

how does someone measure the depth of beauty
love, respect, or patience?

I - Beauty
can the depth of beauty really be measured?
i don't think so . . . it's all subjective
if so, how does a blind man
measure the depth
of the beauty of a flower?
by its aroma, texture, length, color, or the lack there of?
it's like asking someone to define how green is green

II- Love
nor can the depth of love be measured
it cannot be measured
in inches, grams, or ounces
or by some invisible measuring cup
nor can it be measured
by the amount of smiles, sex, or kisses
or how often one is missed
once real love is given it will last forever
even though you may not be
with that person today
it will still exist in the ether
of that person's memories . . .
undefined

Measurements

III - Respect

nor can the depth of respect be measured
like beauty and love, respect cannot be measured
not even by someone's empathy, generosity
appearance, or existence
it cannot be measured by the number of hugs and smiles
text, likes, responses, or emails received
or the number of calls, pats on the back
or any kind of recommendation
nor can respect be measured
by the lack of lies told to one's face
is admiring someone's qualities, skills, abilities
aptitude, motivation, inclinations, or achievements . . .
considered to be respect?
you still won't-don't-can't guarantee that you will
respect anyone
or they you
you just might be secretly jealous of them, or they you
respect cannot be measured
by the appearance of someone regarding one's
feelings, wishes, rights, or traditions
in the end, iron sharpens iron
you know that you know
when respect is given or received
no grins, smiles, or explanation are needed
or require

Measurements

(Continued)

IV - Patience

can the depth of patience be measured?
the depth of patience cannot be measured
but we still wait . . . seconds, minutes, hours, days
weeks, months, and years
for patience to be determined, defined, debated
denied, endured, recognized, restored, revealed
reviewed, and ignored
or not observed at all
because patience is always subjective
and is only real to the imagination
of the person calmly watching . . .
and patiently waiting . . .
to be called

PUPPY LOVE BEGINNINGS

(for Earline Davis)

puppy love beginnings
occupied many sleepless nights
while my silence
never found the right words
to tell her that
"you were my first love"
though i didn't
realize it at the time

for years
i wondered if it had occurred to her
that the handwritten copy of the lyrics
of the song " a lover's concerto" by the toys
that i had mailed to her
confessed my true feelings for her
when it spoke of the magic of true love . . .

now, every time i here that song
i only think of her
and that summer in Southeast Georgia
when i was twelve
and how my heart still remembers
all the wonderful times we shared

INNOCENT LOVE

at 17
i freely
gave you my love
my innocent love
now you own it
the love of my innocence
it cannot be duplicated
only one moment to a lifetime
you/me/we
will always share it
this moment
of innocence
today . . .
tomorrow . . .
and for all time

UNFINISHED LOVE AFFAIR

as the bumpy ride of a greyhound
heading to Tennessee
carries my love to you
along asphalt paths
laced with farms
and barren trees
wandering thoughts
stop to drink
from the well of reflection . . .
memories of past encounters
lifetimes ago
when we made the decision
to meet on this date
at this time
at this place
to write still another chapter
to our unfinished
love affair

STOLEN MOMENTS

lying here
sharing dreams
wishes, and untold secrets
with diamond smiles
and innocent eyes
that give no pretense
tender touches
with no one near
to hear our quiet voices
stolen moments
that confirm
the true love
that blossomed
when no one
was near
to hear our quiet voices

TOGETHER FOREVER

remembering
the first night we met
how easy it was just to talk to you
your eyes were soft and sad
with disappointment and hurt
but your smile said something else
and in the end
you were still willing to trust
and we became the best of friends
you soon became my everything
from the sun in the morning
to the moon at night
without realizing it
your passion occupied my daydreams at work
and my dreams at night, while i slept
my love for you grew
and began to flow like an unending river
filling oceans deep, and flying higher
than any mountain keep
i imagined being your shadow
throughout the day
and by moonlight at night
it just felt right
your hand in mine
like my heart
has always had you in its sight
and now . . .
it longs for us to be together . . .
forever

SELF ESTEEM

no one taught me how to love myself . . .
when we were growing up
you just went out and existed
without someone having to say that they loved you
if you didn't get any kind of love at all, that was ok
because that was the way it was
if nobody were around to love you, that was ok too
if you didn't have the best house
or the best clothes
or the best foods
that was also ok too
we just had what we had
because there were no other answers for it
other than just being poor, just like everyone else
it was laughable to hear someone complaining
about not being loved, or not having enough food
when the people around you were providing, and loving you
the very best way they knew how
today . . . i always hear people talking about self-esteem
and how someone can take it away
it's called ***"self-esteem"*** fool!
you got to learn that s**t on your own
ain't nobody gonna make you love, or unlove yourself
you got to learn how to love yourself all by yourself, first
before you can love anybody else, you have to love yourself
enough to survive . . . everything!
nobody cares about what's in front of you, next to you, or behind you
you got to be intentional about loving yourself
through every situation . . . through every circumstance . . .
through every relationship
you got to be purposeful about loving yourself . . .
every second . . . of every minute . . . of every hour . . . of every day

IN MY DREAMS

sitting here
thinking about
when
and how we first met
i keep wondering
if
or when
i would ever get to see you again

no matter the time and distance
the days, weeks, months, or years
cannot take away
the memories that we share

i often think about
the last opportunity i had to see you . . .
to come to you
to come where you were
but i did not take that chance
other forces were at play

when we talk on the phone
i remember the pledge we made
a pledge that all families
and some friends make
to each other
that they will always be there
for each other

in a lifetime, i was told
you would be blessed
to end up knowing at least
one true friend . . .
in my dreams . . .
it was always you

DAYDREAM AT 30,000 FEET

was she talking to me?
i saw her eyes . . .
her smile . . .
i saw her lips move
but what did she say?
or was her attention directed at the person
in front of . . .
next to . . .
or behind . . . me?
had i only wished . . .
dreamed . . .
imagined . . .
that i had seen her lips move . . .
her smile greet . . .
her eyes speak . . .
had i only hoped that on this day
she would be the one to say
something . . .
anything . . .
everything . . .
to me . . .
or . . . was it just daydreaming?

101 PEARLS . . . GIVE OR TAKE A FEW

they looked so white
silhouetted by her ebony skin
they just laid there . . . innocently at rest
between the crevasses
gently caressing her soft supple skin
a string of pearls – 101 . . . give or take a few
draped around her long regal neck
and that beautiful, little, black dress
101 pearls . . . give or take a few
just dangling in between
two sensuously soft supple breasts
with her every step, back and forth
they did glisten and sway
gently stroking and caressing her
in every conceivable way
a necklace of ivory pearls
101 . . . it looked to be
with a simple knot tied near the end
101 glistening dew drops . . . and me
just touching and caressing her
wherever they may
if they could talk
just imagine what they would say
once, i saw them resting upon her chest
cuddled around one large voluptuous breast
as they framed that voluptuous mound
i found myself holding my breath
excited by the hidden treasure i had found
my knees grew weak
and i almost testified out loud
i'm sure i would have
had it not been for the unsuspecting crowd

101 Pearls . . . Give Or Take A Few

(Continued)

i cannot remember, for the life of me
the face of that lovely creature
that hypnotized me
just those 101 pearls, are all that i see

often . . . i imagine being one of those pearls
one of those 101 pearls . . . give or take a few
and dream of all the sweet and exotic things
i would do to that tender flesh . . .
things that only one dreams about
but never do
one can only guess

oh, how i wish . . .
how i wish i intimately knew
that ebony queen that wore those jewels
those lovely ivory pearls – all 101 of them . . .
give or take a few

ME AND MY RHYTHM

i think i've lost my rhythm . . .
syncopation has . . .
has just messed up my flow
cause i don't move like i use to
i don't talk the same
and i don't walk the same way, either

i don't even think the same way
i think i just lost my flow
you know what i mean? . . .

i think i've lost my rhythm . . .
i don't poet . . . like i used to do
i keep trying to find it
in my foot, in my feet, and in my meter
but i can't do that
without my rhythm

i can't even sway like i use to
i ain't got that thang
that makes me . . . me
i just ain't got . . . me no more

you seen my rhythm?
i need to find it
cause i don't sleep like i used to
i don't do some things
like i used to do
you see . . .
i-i-i just need to find it

Me And My Rhythm

(Continued)

have you seen it?
you haven't
no! are you sure?
it's a one-of-a-kind thing
i need that rhythm
it makes me who i am

we been flowing since the beginning
me and my rhythm
my rhythm and me
we grew up together
but i haven't seen her for a while, though
and i don't know where i left her
or when she left me

we were so close
my rhythm and me
my rhythm could always speak for me
when i opened my mouth
words just flowed out
she just knew when and what to say
even when i wouldn't, won't, don't
or didn't know how to cooperate

my rhythm could move me
even when i didn't want to be moved
without my rhythm
i don't even know where i'm going
or where i've been
yeah . . . me and my rhythm
we're just like twins
we're a matched pair

Me And My Rhythm

well, if you see her . . .
let her know
that i'm looking for her
you know, my rhythm
she means everything to me

so, if you see her
tell her to come on home
cause i miss my rhythm
and my rhythm is needed over here
my rhythm is wanted and needed so badly!
i need her like a plant that needs water

you know . . .
i just need my rhythm
so, i can get in sync with myself
you know what i mean? . . .

i need my rhythm
so, i can flow like i used to
so, i can think, walk, and talk like i used to
yeah . . . you know what i mean? . . .

man . . . i just need to find my rhythm
so i can get in sync with myself
me and my rhythm
when we are in sync
we're like a fine-tuned watch
that you don't even have to wind
you know what i mean? . . .
me . . . and my rhythm

I CAN FEEL IT

this texas sun burns deep
i can feel it . . .
it has begun
the bleaching of my bones

i can feel it . . .
a single bead of sweat
s-l-o-w-l-y
travelling down my spine . . .
evaporating

the hot, harsh winds blister my flesh
and suffocate my every breath
i can feel it . . .
the sandblasting of my soul

the cold desert night leaves me like ice
with only my hallucinations
to warm me
i can feel it . . .

your water-sweet kisses
upon my swollen, parched lips
my footprints
disappearing
into a sea of sand
leaving no trail . . .
no sign for you to follow
i can feel it . . .

SALUTATIONS

when you all were a young and pretty [niggas]
you said that you would love each other forever
and always

but in truth, those kind words
were just hollow salutations
that you put on cards and letters
that often just disappear in shoe boxes
or into the ether, over time

even when people [niggas] try to adhere
to their moral compass
they tend to leave people so easily
for various reasons . . .
reasons only known to themselves
the same people [niggas] that said that
they would love you forever and always
but often, its only after causing
emotional and financial damage
to you, and all the people [niggas] in your life
before they finally realize the damage was done

sometimes
people [niggas] just up and leave
never telling anyone anything
while some people [niggas] have the nerve to
leave a nice little note, message, or text
explaining their decision
in order to make themselves feel
free of guilt or responsibility
even feeling justified
for walking away with a clear conscience
after taking all that you had . . .
to the last dime

(Continued)

and when it comes to breaking your heart these
people [niggas] always like to say

"you know i love you, but . . ."
"you made me do that to you"
and every time they see your family
they try to rob your loved ones
with excuses, deceit, and new and different lies
often, stealing their faith, their time, their money
as well as draining them of their energy

it is those actions that are the things
that everyone [niggas] remembers
and the scars that people [niggas] leave behind
on your bodies . . . on your minds . . .
and on your souls . . .

the outward scars may eventually fade
but the scars that no one sees
they will last forever

and those salutations
of kindness and love that they gave you . . .
they will just go . . .
unremembered

LOVE IS . . .

love is many things . . .
it is often like a theater drama
like a three-act play
or it can be like a short story
a novel, novelette, or novella
where there is a plot
that arranges the incidents and events
that must take place
the *beginning*
that has the who, what, where, when, and why
or things, which is called the *exposition*
that reveals information about the characters
in the *language, song, or music* of the day
while the *theme* ties the *characters*
and events together
where the main character is called the
protagonist and standing in their way is the
antagonist
all the characters involved side with one or the
other the *middle*
provides a series of *conflicts*
or complications
which results in a *climax* or turning point
and the *ending*
is where the final part of the plot
or the conflict
has been resolved
and then the story ends

(Continued)

one can agree
that sometimes
love may not have an ending
like a play in a theater
that ends after the third act
or like a short story
or like a novel, novelette, or novella
because love can mean
and be experienced in many ways
love can be . . .
. . . physiological, monogamous, bisexual, or optional
. . . cute, calm, innocent, wonderful, and a blessing
. . . speechless, determined, thoughtful, and patient
. . . secure, sensual, sexy, tender, and sensational
. . . bashful, kind, not envious, humble, and selfless
. . . an infatuation, a friendship, or companionate
. . . happiness, laughter, peaceful, almost like family
. . . understanding, listening, being present, sharing
. . . confident, honesty, trusting, and forgiving
. . . respected, persistent, sustained, and enduring
. . . overlooked, unrequited, or ignored
. . . not easy, absence, lonely, and a struggle
. . . a series of breakups and breakthroughs
. . . angry, painful, reflective, and regretful
love can be all these things, and more . . .
however, one thing is for sure . . .
love is . . . not promised

A GOOD DENTIST

i went to the dentist the other day
and when i left
i saw an old friend coming my way
he asked me why i was smiling so hard?
that my smile could be seen
from a mile away
i told him that i was showing him my
brand-new smile
that i felt like
it was a brand-new day
because the dentist
had fixed all of my broken teeth
he smiled in his usual way
and asked
"so, how's the family?"
i told him that they were fine too
but i was even better
cause i finally found myself
a good dentist
to fix all my broken teeth
because being married
was like caring cement blocks
in a backpack
or eating rocks
for an afternoon snack

A SEASONAL DRAMA

sitting here
listen to your insults
to my intelligence
the spitting out of words
vindicating
your one-act masque
critics gave rave reviews
of your extravaganza
but only you knew of its flaws
and secretly hoped that they would go
undetected
caught up in a role so convincing
   (especially to myself)
i thought it unqualified
your seasonal drama
but like the seasons
attitudes/feelings change uncovering
the sculpture
carved in old snow disclosing
the beauty and the ugliness
of relationships . . . politics . . .
and reality

THE JOY OF UGLY FEET

i have this thing for feet . . .
ugly feet that is
everybody was born with pretty feet
nice and smooth to the touch
but as you get older
they get uglier and uglier
you know the kind
the ones with the automatic corn on the baby toe
a bunion here . . . a callus there
screaming for a pedicure
little feet, fat feet, long or skinny feet
some rough, some tough
and some ashy ones too
but most of the time
they just be looking rough
you know what i mean?
it's not that i don't like pretty feet . . .
pretty feet just don't do nothing for me
i would imagine
that they do have their place though
but from ugly feet
you can learn the most from
laugh the hardest at
moan the loudest because of
and complain the most about . . .
shoes too small, too big, too new
and don't forget the old shoes
and the hand-me-down shoes
you see, ugly feet have a history
they have seen it all
and they have survived to tell
"their" story
rough, tough, ugly feet

A FEW GOOD MEN

(For Hubert and Jack Givens)

the bible says:
"the steps of a good man are ordered by the lord,
and he delighteth in his way"
"though he may fall, he shall not be utterly cast down,
for the lord upholds him with his hand"

so, i search and traveled far
over land and sea, and sometimes by car
in search of examples of a good man
but only a few good men did i find, or see
who could compare to those men
who had stood right in front of me

in all my days, only a few men stood out to me:
men who were quiet, discrete, and slow to anger
men who understood selfless service, and intestinal fortitude
men whose good works spoke to their righteous character
men whose word was his bond
and no one could remember a curse word being said
or a selfish thing ever being done
men who chose to be good men
and did the right thing
when no eyes were upon them

men who were servant leaders
placing the needs and interests of others
before their own self-interests and needs

men who sacrificed themselves
as their Lord would want
for those who could not help themselves
men who were not afraid of evil tidings
because their hearts were fixed
trusting in their Lord

A Few Good Men

(Continued)

men who were a brave sailor
and a courageous Marine
men who sacrificed their lives for their fellow man
when violence and injuries found them in vietnam
their Lord recognized his sons
and sent them home to begin their life again

men who were obedient sons
loving husbands, fathers, and protective brothers
resolute grandsons, uncles, and nephews
kind coworkers, and a friend to all

men who did the right thing
at every opportunity
for all others in their community

my soul is troubled
and my tears flow like a mountain stream because
the news has come
that we have lost both of these good men
men that meant so much to me

who will stand in their place?
who will fill their shoes?
who will tell their stories of love
sacrifice, service, and dedication . . .

who will tell their story . . .?
the story of the best men i have ever known . . .
who will tell their story?
. . . other than me

SLOUCH PEOPLE

the reason why
people who have
the ability
yet fail to aspire to great things
and/or achieve success
is that these individuals are usually surrounded
by *"slouchy people"* that contribute nothing
to the positive growth
of that individual
feeding on them
like leeches
until there is nothing left
for that person to aspire to, or with
financially
physically
or mentally
when someone asks . . .

> *"what happened?"*
> *"he was so gifted and talented"*
> *"i wonder why he didn't succeed?"*

these *"slouchy people"* reply . . .

> *"i dunno, i did all that i could do to help!"*

THE ORGINAL PIPE DREAM

from the beginning of reconstruction
they thought they were free . . .
free from the chains of oppression
soon their so-called freedom
turned into a new and different
kind of oppression
so, they developed a new and different kind
of obsession
in their continual search for real freedom
some turned to *"moonshine" and gin* some
turned to "*brown licka*"
some turned to them *"bones"*
some turned to the *"pleasures of the flesh"*
some turned to *"chewin' tobacco"*
some turned to *"snuff,"*
and then some turned to the *"opium pipes"*
and learned how to puff, puff, pass . . . while
they searched, worked, and smoked they
continued to ignore their situations wishing
they were someplace else . . . dreaming of
being free
in between the unknown addictions
of various drugs, alcohols, and opioids some
recovered
while others continued to smoke and puff . . .
still searching for whatever their pleasure
soon, their hopes faded in the smoke . . .
or faded in their veins . . .
where they thought they were finally free

still others
from generation after generation
continued dreaming of new ideas and
new plans to achieve freedom year
after year
those dreams just proved to be
a dream deferred
or an impossible dream
that had never really materialized
still, they hoped for a freedom . . .
with no violence . . .
no prejudice . . .
no discrimination . . .
no racial marginalization . . .
dreams of equality . . .
dreams of equal opportunity . . .
in the end
after centuries of struggles
those constant streams
of new ideas, hopes, and dreams . . .
dreams of a real freedom kept
coming . . . and going
hopes and dreams
that originated in the smoke
from an opium pipe
the original "*pipe dream*"
of real freedom

LES MCCANN: LIVE AT THE HOBBIT

Les is just a man . . . big
in mind and spirit
you could say he was built for comfort
not for speed
but when the piano man begins to play
his fingers magically
strokes and caresses those ivory keys
the sound made by felt-covered hammers
striking metal . . . strings
sends out a supernatural transcontinental vibe
like no other
the sensation is like . . . traveling
at the speed of sound
"and the world around you
melts into a syncopated blur"
as Eddie Harris kicks it into warp drive

as he plays . . .
his body rocks and sways
building momentum
and his fingers . . . like pistons
making 4/4 time . . .
and his fuel becomes the applause
made by two objects coming together
rhythmically moving him/us through
time and space

Les McCann: Live At The Hobbit

(Continued)

the endless . . . 1-2 nighters
are beginning to show
on his face . . . and hands
but not his music
it's still timeless, original, innocent, and pure and
his voice still has that fire
that makes your fingers . . . snap . . .
and pop
and your feet . . . go . . . pitty-pat
and your head . . . be-bop
up and down
and sway from side to side

if you get the chance to ask him how he does it
he'll tell you, as he told a young novice

> *"one needs only compare its relativity of the focus*
> *that one has when one is to trying to make it . . .*
> *real"*

nodding his head in revelation, the young novice
responded, shaking his head like he finally understood . . .

> *"humm . . . focus . . . yeah . . . trying to make it real . . .*
> *yeah . . . i can dig that . . . yeah man . . . focus . . . yeah . . .*

then he hesitates and asks . . .

> *"compared to what?"*

The Hobbit, Southeast 52nd Street Portland, Oregon, Album: Swiss Movement - Compared to What: Les McCann Piano, Eddie Harris Tenor - Sax; Benny Baily - Trumpet; Donald Dean - Drums; Leroy Vinegar – Bass

GIRLS NIGHT OUT – Just Above The Smoke

one sister
crying
two sisters
comforting
three sisters
drinking
four sisters
dancing
five sisters
laughing
while the jazz flowed
just above the smoke
and the bar tender yawned
while all the listeners
snapped their fingers
and tapped their feet
to the down beat

JAZZMERIZED

my skin just slid off.
i couldn't even stop it. i
just sat there, hypnotized,
glassy-eyed, and bare to
the bone.
as they played,
i listened . . . helpless and
unknowing.
all i could do was smile,
shake my head,
from side to side,
and pat my feet
to the down beat.

3/1989 - Les McCann & Eddie Harris, Live at The Hobbit, SE 52nd Street / 32 nd Street and Holgate Blvd., Portland, Oregon

Wide Open Magazine," Summer 1991 Annual Issue, Wide Open Magazine, Santa Rosa, CA

POLYPHONIC RHYTMS

*(Upon listening to Mel Brown's Quintet
at The HOBBIT in Portland, OR)*

they were sharp
sharp as swiss cheddar
and we feasted like fat rats
in an audible cheese factory
all we could do was
listen
snap our fingers
and smile
till our fingers got sore
and our face muscles
got tired

"The Independent Review," Page 55, Summer 1989, The
Independent Review, Kingsville, MO

A CHILD WAITING

i am just a child . . .
a motherless child
waiting . . .
a fatherless child
wishing . . .

i am just a child wanting praying,
and waiting
for someone to come . . .
for someone to understand
my story

i have always been
just a child wanting . . .
praying . . . and wishing . . .
wishing for someone to care . . .

i have always been
waiting for someone to come . . .
waiting for someone to understand
my sorrow
my struggle
my frustrations
and my shame . . .

it has always been
a story of sorrow and shame
not anger
cause it's too late for anger

A Child Waiting

(Continued)

does anyone know how it is
to be overlooked . . .
looked passed . . .
for someone taller . . . smaller
someone more handsome . . .
for someone plainer . . .
for someone prettier

was i not tall enough?
was i not young enough?
was i not white enough?
was i not black enough?
is loving someone based on weight
height, age, gender, or race?

no one can know
the lies that i have lived with
waiting for someone to return
the hope wished for
waiting for someone to look my way

the unrequited loves
that have come my way
siphoning the water
from the roots of my soul
leaving me like chipped ice
that stands alone . . . once more
hopeful, bright, and lucent
only to evaporate
and fade away . . .
unknown

THE ORPHAN:
THE COLOR OF EXPERIENCE I

we all have an opinion about people
like most people do
but everyone's opinion about you
is nothing new
they say you're like this
or maybe you're like that
some say they care . . .
and some say they love you . . .
some have no faith . . .
and some just up and leave
and never come back
so, people really don't know
the real you . . . the real facts
and why you act the way you act

they don't know how you felt when
you learned that you were
whisked away in a blanket
when it was discovered
that you were an unwanted child
and they/we/you
will never have all the facts
so, their opinion really doesn't matter
and that's ok
cause that's in the past
and you hate looking back

but the color of experience
can tell you sooo much more
about who you really are

THE ORPHAN:
THE COLOR OF EXPERIENCE II

they really don't know
the kindnesses or inhumane traumas
issued, received, or committed on you because
of your relentless pursuit
of success
your thirst for knowledge
your correct speech
or your light skin complexion
and your curly hair

i wonder who your daddy is
i bet they will never know
where you've been
or what you've seen
or the many things
that was done to you
and the things that you had to
suffer, endure, and to overcome
in the name of equality . . . romance . . .
and danger . . .
or just having fun

but the color of experience
can tell you sooo much more
about who your really are

THE ORPHAN: THE COLOR OF EXPERIENCE III

i wonder who your momma is?
cause she will never know anything
about the reasons for your attitude . . .
your aptitude . . . your abilities . . .
your inclinations . . . your creativity . . .
or your motivations . . .

she will only see
or hear
about your experiences
on tv
or on the radio
from your friends and foes
as they constantly talk
about your highs and lows

people only see you smile
that cheshire cat smile
but behind that smile
they will never know
what actually moves you . . .
or why

but the color of experience
can tell you sooo much more
about who you really are

THE ORPHAN:
THE COLOR OF EXPERIENCE IV

people will never know
that you had wandered near and far
over land and sea . . .
by bus, train, plane, boat, and car . . .
always searching and sacrificing
to get you here, to where you are
because they were all blind
to your ups and downs
it's amazing how you kept your right mind
as they continue to remain curious
about your ability to still remain
generous and kind

they will never know the origin
of your feelings of emptiness
and that place that holds the memories
that often makes you cry, grimace, and frown

they will never know the impact
of your lost surrogate mothers
fathers, friends, and your close acquaintances
that can no longer be found
but their loving memories still seem to hang around

but the color of experience
can tell you sooo much more
about who you really are

THE ORPHAN: THE COLOR OF EXPERIENCE V

they will never know about
your feelings of mistrust
and sometimes being without purpose . . .
without direction
and your nagging desire
of just wanting to be alone
so, you could have some *"real"* peace

they will never understand the simple fact that
there were many obstacles
and many of the challenges were large
and some were small
that you always persevered
and overcame them all

that there were many achievements
and some successes
some were large
and some were also small
but in the end
they were unsung
or ignored

they just didn't care
or, maybe
they were just bored and tired
after all

but the color of experience
can tell you sooo much more
about who you really are

THE ORPHAN:
THE COLOR OF EXPERIENCE VI

they will never understand
that in the back of your mind
you knew the reasons were all related
no matter what explanations
or excuses that were constantly stated
because you understood
that you would never be white enough
or black enough
for them . . . yourself . . . or for any other place
that you would ever call home
and to this day, for some reason
you are still misunderstood
and often hated
and this is why you still must stand alone
to remain strong . . . to endure . . .
and to overcome

in the end . . . the color of experience
always tells you sooo much more
about who you really are

I KNOW YOU LOVE ME

look at me once, so my heart can smile.
don't walk away without that smile . . .
that smile that calls me to follow.

i know you love me,
though you might forget sometimes.
i remember you carried me for 9 months . . .
i remember you cleaned too many houses . . .
i remember you worked in too many restaurants,
and cleaned too many offices . . .

i remember you put a roof over my head
clothes on my back, and food on the table
just so i could have something to eat, every day.
i remember you did all of that,
until i could do it for myself.

when you gently touch my face,
my heart remembers that soft, gentle,
soothing, touch of my mother.
when you come close,
my heart knows your name . . .
the name of my mother . . .
the name that all women are compared to.
because i am your son,
don't you know that my life is yours?
you will always be my moon, and my universe.

i hope you know what you mean everything to me,
and you mean everything to my heart . . .
to my heart, and my life . . .
because they will always be yours . . .
until the day i die.

AT TWENTY-FIVE

at 25
the youth within
silently rebelled
as she instructed/chastised
me
on the error of my ways
when she had finished
i felt an angry voice
growing inside
suddenly
i heard an
acquiescent voice say
"yes ma'am"

FALL PERSON

when bonita told louis
he was a
"fall person"
louis impetuously protested
and said
"i'm a man for all seasons!"
bonita just smiled
as she reached into his pockets
and pulled out
a hand full of leaves

SAX

Sax
is his own man
he's not caught up
in the confusion
between independence
and dependency
to him
there is no difference
Sax
some people say
is . . . you know
but most are afraid to ask
however
Sax
simply doesn't care
to him
all things are relative
because perceptions are real
"only"
to the individual
. . . ain't that right *Sax?*

1990 American Poetry Annual, March 1990,
The Amherst Poetry Society, Baltimore, MD

TIMES LIKE THESE

they say . . .
when you have lived . . . lived your life . . . fully
and have grown old and worn – gracefully

it becomes time . . .
a time to talk of what could have been
and what will be missed

a time to talk of missed adventures, past relations
and to make amends with family and life-long friends

a time to talk of love's past, your children's children
and the journeys you attempted, but did not make
to talk of wars, service, and how we made America great

a time to accept the fact that sometimes
some things are stronger than the body/mind/will admit

it becomes time . . .
to remember Saturday matinees, icescapes, carnivals
circuses, cotton candy, and caramel apples on a stick

a time to be patient for patient's sake
and not complain when you're feeling ill or sick
to make peace with yourself, and to quietly wait . . .
a time when some people want us . . . expect us
to contribute more than our fair share
to sit still and smile – discreetly
and wait . . .
wait until they can get to us

a time when we have grown old and worn – gracefully
and have learned how to do many things well
to hold our breath, and to discretely smile. . .
and be silent ,when they start talking about rest homes
social security . . . medicare . . . viruses . . . and death

RACIAL INJUSTICE

the declaration of independence stated:
"a nation in which there would be equal justice for all"
echoing the vision of a just and equitable society
more than two hundred years later
it has yet to be achieved
without equality, true justice cannot occur although
generations of civil rights activism
have put a dent in the legal, political, social educational
and other spheres
but the institution of slavery, maltreatment of immigrants
and the forced removal of indigenous peoples
marked the beginnings of a system of racial injustice
from which our country has yet to break free
i can stand it – for a little while
but to keep overlooking the personal dignity of any man
especially, *"the black man"*
will not have a good end
i will give you a quick answer to the "*question*"
"what are we going to do about the race question?" you
really don't want an answer to that "*question*" especially
when you continue to support and label racist white
organizations, white nationalist, white supremist KKK
skin heads, etc., as *"good people"*
and then you label black people
or black organizations that peacefully march and protest
and support the cause as combative, and aggressive
organizations that typically favor extreme violence, or
confrontational methods, or as thugs, or violent people,
criminals, hooligans, and gangsters

i will give you my opinion to the answer to the "*question*"
not in words, but of pure energy and action that will only
end with total devastation of this systemic racism that you
hold so dear; a response that you seem to not understand
because society continues to support the same point of
view that you have grown and fostered for over 400 years
so, stop asking that "*racist question,*" in the first place
educate yourself; do something with that white privilege
of yours; read something; volunteer; hire people of color;
do anything positive to improve this deep-seated idea of
systemic racism and inequities that has always
disadvantaged communities of color

A PICTURE ROCKWELL NEVER PAINTED

(A poem for Ricky Rouse)

motionless
he watches . . .
a piece of sunlight
sifting through the window
of sandwich sized bars
that makes checkerboard shadows
across his body
as wind-blown scents
permeate his senses
and disturbs old spider webs
and stagnant dust particles
that occupy his cell . . . his soul
his only thought . . .
"i wonder why normal rockwell never painted . . .
this part of America?"

FAMILY REUNION

what will you say
to the future generations?
will you lie and say
you just did not have the time to visit . . .
to celebrate . . .
to remember . . .
those who came before us?
that you knew nothing
of their joys and struggles
their heartaches
and their determination
to survive and endure
no matter the cost
will you say . . . we didn't have time . . .
we were too tired . . .
we did not have the money . . .
we did not want to know *"those"* people . . .
what excuse will you use today
when they ask you tomorrow . . .
where do we come from?
who were our people?
what do you remember about our kin? . . .
our ancestors? . . . our family? . . .
what were they like?
did they look like me?
what will you tell your children
when they say . . .
you can remember
everything about our
friends and neighbors
but why don't you remember
anything about us?

FIVE ON THE BLACK HAND SIDE

give me some dap
when you say hello
give me some dap
before you go
give me one of them fives
no change please
give it to me down low
but not on my knees
give me some dap
give me a five up high
no fist bump please
don't give me no mess
you know, give me five
come on, don't be too slow
give me five everywhere i go
but i like a five
on the black hand side, the best
slide it to me easy
this ain't no test
tell me something i don't know
tell me the place i need to go
tell me something about something
before you go
give me five for the cause
give it to me strong
this ain't no test
let me know you know
cause five on the black hand side
is always better than the rest
you know what i mean . . .

my brother!

SAFE SPACE

when the real revolution comes
what will you do my brother?
when the real revolution comes
what will you do my sister?
what side will you be on?
what side . . . black or white?
or will you be confused
do you think that a college degree will save you?
do you think that interracial
mocha, caramel, chocolate, or pecan tan
color of yours will make you safe?
if so, you will be sorely disappointed
don't you know that the one drop rule still applies?

what will you do when the real revolution comes?
whose side will you be on . . .
when there is no middle ground?
will you be on the side of your family? your black family? . . .
or will you be with your un/known white family?

what will you do when betrayal and slander occur?
what will you do when they come to make fruit
to hang from their poplar tree?
what will you do when the police dog, tear gas and real bullets fly?
where will you go? . . . what will you do? . . . where will you hide? . . .
<— for whites only   for coloreds only —>
it's a real question; my soul brothers and sisters
think about it . . . what side will you be on?
where will your safe space be
when the real revolution comes?

BUILDERS OF NATIONS

they were free black men of color
you may not have recognized them
for they carried the look of many
strong, proud, and majestic black men
and women strong in nature
proud in character
and majestic in carriage
their fathers were free men too
though bound by society
they were still free in spirit
and like their fathers before them
they were fathers of many talents
they were fathers of many nations
beyond the challenges of bondage
and inhumane sacrifices
discrimination, marginalization, and
racial injustice, they educated their children . . .
and they educated them well they
were the fathers of many . . .
masons, scientists, lawyers, physicians
of soldiers, sailors, and marines
of people of high finance
of teachers, engineers, and artists
of dentists, electricians, and butchers
of social workers, actors, and nurses

Builders of Nations

of farmers, bookkeepers, and carpenters
of architects, gardeners, and scientists
of lifeguards, plumbers, and ditch diggers
of bakers and software developers
of opticians, librarians, and auto mechanics
of singers, dancers, and radio and tv personalities
of field workers, hairdressers, and barbers
of painters, mail carriers, and construction workers
of secretaries, pharmacists, and journalists
of analysts, veterinarians, and dietitians
of philosophers, economists, and bus driver
of pilots and air traffic controllers
of judges, manufacturers, and managers
of chefs, firefighters, and poets
of real estate brokers and designers . . .
many or any profession will do
remember . . .
a drop of blood will make you black
so look around you . . .
and open your eyes and see . . .
behold!
a black man did that!

SEOUL II: PROGRESS

stagnant 20th century smog stands motionless
as it watches over this oriental city
standing motionless like slow death
that knows how to sit and wait . . .

rainbow smog-clouds change colors
with my every movement
as the thought . . .
"the EPA would have a field day in this place." . . .
crosses my mind

entering the city through one of the ancient gates
i past the stone sentries
and immediately find myself being caught up
in an audible force field of 8 million souls
all in a rush to go nowhere . . .
the country is surrounded by water
on three sides
and communism on the fourth
like the masses, i make my way
shoulder to shoulder
through the mass-transit traffic jams
wondering . . .
"what will it be like when the electronic highways,
skyscrapers, skywalks, super-trains, and
underground subways are finished?"
just one long-long-long people jam! . . .
a voice answers

like ants, single in purpose, as they move forward within
this state-of-the-art, twenty-first century modal
surrounded and covered by self-contained
internally pressurized, seasonally controlled positronic
stimulated, hi-tech metal structures
that will hide and eliminate the natural elements

what price is to be extracted
for this thing called progress? . . .
what benefit to humankind?
what or who will survive its wake?
what enduring legacy will remain?

the true desires of these people – this nation
is unknown to me
but i do know that this thing called *"progress"*
like weeds
has begun to choke the ancient landmarks
into submission

in seoul, only a few smog-stained monuments
seem to have survived . . .
and this multi-colored smog that stands . . . motionless
this shroud of smog that sits and waits patiently
for progress

THE VISTORS

it was his people's naïve generosity which allowed
the overpowering need of the *"visitors"* to impose their
will and their culture upon the nation . . .
and its people
it was the visitor's greed, deceit, and broken promises
cleverly disguised as change and progress
that brought centuries of discord to his land . . .
the land of his ancestors
in the beginning, the changes were small, subtle, and
noble but when the news spread about these peaceful and
uncomplicated people, the armies quickly came spreading
a new version of change and progress . . . harvesting its
treasures and resources
leaving nothing in return . . .
except war, destruction, and servitude
and now . . .
what was once a familiar place with familiar customs and
friendly faces was now strange, foreign, and unknown he
felt lost, as if he were a "visitor"
in his own land
so now . . .
any "visitor" is met with caution and a measure of disdain
his valley was not on the Korean National Tourism Circuit
of *"Things To See"*
in fact, it was out of the way
and that is how the old man would like to keep it
to him a visitor . . . any visitor
was just another *"foreigner"*
a suspect who brings greed, deceit, and broken promises
cleverly disguised as change and progress

IN THE VALLEY OF THE THREE PEAKS

each day the old man meets the sun
and from the banks of the rice fields, he watches the seedling
growing in mass, scrutinizing with grey eyes
each bundle, each stem, each leaf
for its readiness for planting

with sweat, sickle, and hoe he has carved out his life's blood
steps in the mountain side that will ensure his existence
for another year

he is not a farmer, but a master of irrigation and survival life
lessons learned from his father, and him from his father

when the air is right, and the shadow rest at the edge
of the paddy fields, then, and only then, will it be time to plant

each day he will watch the planters come and go
he will head home, only after inspecting each planted row
each field, for perfection

throughout the season, the old man will come and
inspect his rice crop and survey the land that has
become his life's blood
and on each tomorrow, and each day after, the old man
will rise in the cold morning darkness, and make his way
up the kimchi path to meet the sun, until his fields have
turned golden, and the harvest is complete

(Continued)

as one season gives way to the next, the old man will
gather his sons and they their sons, to sit around the
family fire, as his fathers had done with him

they will share the "hanjongshik" – a plain and simple
meal of vegetables, eggs, fish, and other kimchi dishes,
made of pickled and fermented cabbages, cucumbers,
and turnips, along with soup and rice of the season

when their stomachs are full, they will drink the tea
of the ginseng root, and the milky white home-made
makkoli rice wine

later into the night, the joyful chatter will cease, and all
eyes will focus on the old man, as he beings to re-tell the
stories passed on by his fathers

he will tell of the cold rains, hot suns, strong winds
and great wars

he will talk of the mongolian and japanese intruders and
how they brought change to the land

and inevitably, he will pass on the secrets of survival in
the valley of the three peaks
where the mornings are calm, and the mist clings to the
mountains, as dew to the leaves

AT THE WATER'S EDGE

standing at the edge of the mediterranean
listening to the screams of angry waves
relentless in their attack on the rocks and boulders
beneath my feet

fluid fingers of foam
dart in and out of craggy spaces
that only they can reach
as tiny pearl/black and sand/brown barnacles
open and close their shells
welcoming the force that is both life and death while
winged sentinels on patrol stand close by vigilantly
watching . . . waiting

the moment brings a warm sun to my neck
a cool breeze to my face
and the roar of a thousand voices to placate me
as my chest rises and falls like the waves below
i am hypnotized by a clorox/green sea
that reaches up to touch
and tempt me with a kiss

on the beach . . .
a lone sandpiper takes time-out
from a game of tag with the winter waves
to watch . . .
an off-season jogger passing by . . .
a strolling beachcomber lost in thought
searching for a treasure of coins lost by mermaids . . .
and an old woman in a straw hat, shawl, sandals
and a faded pink sun dress
her face is pink too
as pink as the flowers laced around her straw hat . . .

At The Water's Edge

(Continued)

gradually
the old woman stops, removes her sandals
and walks slowly to the water's edge . . . and waits

in time, a wave reaches her
she crinkles up her toes in the wet sand . . .
and smiles
then . . . i smile too

as i turn to leave
sand crabs scurry between the rocks seeking shelter from my shadow
the sandpiper returns to his never-ending
game of tag
while a large multi-colored sea gull
fights off his comrades
hovering over his prize delivered by the sea

sometimes . . .
it is comforting to know
that no matter where you live
that some things will remain unchanged
that on tomorrow
the wind will continue to blow
the tides will continue to ebb and flow
and that on tomorrow
the sandpiper will continue to play tag . . .
beachcombers will walk the beach . . . searching . . .
little old ladies will crinkle up their toes
in the wet sand . . .
and the sea gulls will be on patrol . . .
watching . . . and waiting . . .
for another soul to stand hypnotized
at the water's edge

VIEW FROM THE MEZZANINE

in a silent daze, i walk the halls, ride the elevators
and contemplate the well-being of my children, divorce,
death, and the phases of institutional beginnings and
endings, and the complexity and nuances of social
interactions

silently the elevator moves . . .
before me stand two cute little pixies – too young . . .
with ruby red lips – too small . . . in blue jeans – too large
both lost, confused, and afraid of adult first impressions
and the thought of sharing erotically confined spaces

two elderly women stare at my steel reflection
nervously clutching their bags, and each other
and behind the young nymphs
a red faced, overweight businessman
entertains himself with change from a dollar
and a game of pocket pool in oversized pockets

as the elevator door opens, the eyeball silence gives way
to a kaleidoscope of noise, music, and open conversations
i feel dazed, as my olfactory senses are bombarded by
a suffocating rush of artificial smells, sights, and sounds
with nowhere to escape, i take a break on the *"Mezzanine"*

at the outside café, a glass of orange juice – 100% pure
(made from concentrate) that must be shaken violently
before consumption, is the order of the day
unconscientiously . . .
i notice the echoes of piano sounds in the distance . . .

View From The Mezzanine

(Continued 2 of 3)

and from the mezzanine, i sit and watch . . .
the female servers, as they work the room
for gratuities, casting seductive smiles and gentle touches
upon weary patrons

my senses begin to monitor a distant piano solo
and networking businessmen, seeking an edge
as they slowly become consumed by 12 fluid ounces . . .
of alcohol and themselves

the tv broadcasts subliminal visual manifestations
of eccentric people, shoes, and beer commercials . . .
commercials of talking bulls; frogs; and dogs; flying shoes
and delicious fig-leaf ladies from sports illustrated; ESPN;
two young rough necks, with talent, discussing an eight-
figure deal; Nike, Reebok, Michael, the NY Knicks, and the
Dallas Cowboys; and other addictive creations of the
imagination written, produced, and directed by a new breed
of brash marketing demons *(another name for white collar
crooks)* searching and surfing the electronic waves from
Portland to Japan for that *"special something"* parents want
to see, and every young kid wants to be

down below . . .
two slick latin-lovers trade seductive glances with a crowded
tabled of hawk-nosed jewish princesses, and words neither of
them understands
while both try to escape into each other's v-neck crevices
behind beguiling, polite smiles that promise exotic pleasures

View From The Mezzanine

(Continued 3 of 3)

close by. . .
three "*good catholic girls*" chain smoke
and sip gin while they discuss biological clocks
and flirt with three asian men with ginseng
floating in their pockets

the piano solo ceases. . . and begins again
and the fires of a restive spirit begin to unfold
noticing that the ice in my orange juice has shed its cold tears
upon a wet napkin that heralds several use-less and unsung
products of the day

restlessly, my body begins to move. . .
soon . . .
a well-manicured hand gently caresses my arm
as a sensuously seductive voice inquires
"*is there anything else 'i' can get for you?*"
my orange juice, and my breath, are whisked away
as i consider her offer
but an instinctive, yet reluctant
"*not today*" is my only reply
retracing my steps, i attempt to leave . . .

i reach the elevator . . .
but the echo of another piano solo saturates my soul
i am compelled by the melody to take another break . . .
to take another transitory view of the world
from the "*Mezzanine*"
and contemplate the well-being of my children, divorce, death
and the phases of institutional beginnings . . . and endings . . .
and of the complexity and nuances of social interactions

THE TROLLEY

(New Orleans)

once the trolley winds its way down
Canal Street
through the loop of the hotel district
it makes its way around the oxbow
down passed st. Charles Street
near the edge of the Vieux Carré
the old square
it traces and retraces the cobble stone route
of the Three Sisters, Baucus, and the
Tchoupitoulas passing the Grandstand and
Lafayette square methodically clicking along
enroute to the Mississippi
a couple of joggers, and a bicycling ghetto
acrobat mock the trolley's cadence
as it keeps time with the crickets and katydids
occasionally stopping to gain a passenger or
two the ride is steady, and deliberate
slow and easy
the trolley always keeps its promise though
it doesn't boast on saving you time
it just promises to get you there
the trolley is meant to get you to your
destination in one piece
but at no certain time, the big easy way . . .
deliberate . . . steady . . . slow . . . and easy

IN THE COOL OF THE TWILIGHT

in the utah evening twilight
a cool spring breeze raises the hair on my neck as
evening birds start to sing
as the silhouettes of the uinta mountain range that
runs east to west
and wasatch mountain range
that runs west and north, watch over me

in the cool of the twilight, the mountain ranges
remind me of the knuckles of a hand
the ridges and valleys extend like
fingers that touch the edge of the city

when people say, *"this is god's country"*
i know now what they mean
i am gazing upon the hands of god and
i feel so infinitely unimportant among
these giants of stone
so swift, majestic, and strong to be in
awe of their creation is the correct state
of mind to be in

as a cool spring breeze raises the hair
on my neck evening birds start to sing
as the silhouettes of mountains
watch over me
in the cool of the evening twilight

DOWN AT THE SEASIDE

down at the seaside
at the end of lewis and clark
the roar of the ice-cold blue/green ocean
greets the land-locked pioneers
long after it has grown dark
they seem almost heroic in their quest
resolved to put the cruel harsh winds
and an unwilling pacific sun to the test

some seek their fortune in search of seashells
sand dollars and logs adrift
while others try their hand at peddling beads
trinkets, taffy, and caramel corn

only the rugged, courageous, and brave like
beached whales needing to be saved bare
their pale bodies/souls
to the harsh wind and blistering sun
with sincere hopes that they will be blessed
with a little fun in the sun
or even an ebony pecan tan
they almost appear desperate
like new jersey junkies trying to get a fix
anyway they can

Down At The Seaside

(Continued)

the setting sun, and the sea, with her lost voices
indifferent to their causes
watches . . .
and fails to applaud
these pale descendants of Oregon pioneers
only to reward their efforts
with distain and blisters
full of misery and pain

in the evening mist
treasure hunters and swollen bodies
leave their trails in the sand
like methodical giant sea turtles . . . exhausted
as they return to their beach homes
offices, orchards, farms, and homesteads

tomorrow . . . at sunrise
others will begin their annual quest . . .
their pilgrimage to the oregon coast
until they reach the sandy shores
of the only *"beach"* they will ever know
the beach known as *"seaside"*
at the end of the lewis and clark trail
where the roar of the ice-cold
blue/green pacific ocean
crashes, moves, and flows . . .
long after it has grown dark

CONVENIENT TO IGNORE . . . HARD TO FORGET

it's convenient to ignore how, as a child, you enjoyed playing in the cool summer rain, floating popsicle sticks and paper sailboats along the curbside; chasing/catching raindrops on your tongue; jumping into the middle of every rain puddle you could find, even though you were told to *"stay out of the water puddles," but b*eing young, innocent, and happy are the memories that are never hard to forget.

it's convenient to ignore how it must feel to hunger/thirst and want peace of mind/spirit; to watch the beauty/youth/hope perish before your eyes, until the skin turns to leather, and every rib/bone can be counted without effort. but the emptiness of hollow eyes and parched faces . . . abject poverty, disease, malnutrition, starvation, death, and what those things will make one do to survive, is never hard to forget.

it's convenient to ignore the violations and transgressions committed by/on your fellow man, and how the politicians make excuses and give speeches filled with rhetorical comments, questions, and answers that tactfully close your/my/our minds eye to the truth; and how so many righteous, religious, and everyday people are so willing to pretend / ignore / accept seeing people without . . . faces / color / possessions. especially, when they're not one of them, but an untruth . . . a lie . . . an injustice, no matter where/when/how it is committed, is never hard to forget.

Convenient To Ignore . . . Hard To Forget

(Continued 2 of 5)

it's convenient to ignore where, when, and how you discover the difference between puppy love and lust, and how you thought . . . puppy love was nice, but lust felt so much better; but everyone knows that puppy love . . . any true love, is never hard to forget.

it's convenient to ignore the 70% of people who lived in a Cincinnati's city within a city – *"the west end projects: the lincoln courts; the laurel holmes; park town; over the rhine; and the stanley rowe towers."* all of them beautiful and poor, but proud; how they struggled to *"balance"* living in two cultures; and how you hated white/black . . . strangers for saying *"i just can't believe it – you speak so well," a*s if you had recently learned to speak the English language; or for petting you on the head, in their feeble attempt, to sample the curly texture of your hair, only to watch their face grimace with disgust, or smile with surprise when they found no grease on their palms, and the fact that the soft texture of your hair was *"natural;"* and how their eyes/faces lit up with acceptance, as if they were giving you their permission for being who you were - me; or those white faces resenting you for having something you were not entitled to; but the contempt for blatant ignorance, or subtle bigotry, committed by anyone, is never hard to forget.

it's convenient to ignore the numbness that accompanies the news of the birth of you first born; the death of the guy that was supposed to be your father; his mother, and your half-sister - all on the same day; in addition, your mother's brothers - your favorite uncles; her mother – your grandma; but the beginning and ending of amazing lives shared together is never hard to forget.

Convenient To Ignore . . . Hard To Forget

(Continued 3 of 5)

it's convenient to ignore the summer heat, fire hydrants, public swimming pools full of chlorine, and ashy little brown bodies . . . 4th of July picnics, fireworks, firecrackers, and the cherry bomb that exploded in your hand . . . the anger, the blisters, and the pain that followed; then asking yourself, in disgust, "why?" . . . why do black people "celebrate" independence Day, in the first place? and the fact that in a lifetime of searching, no one ever voiced, nor did you ever find, a real, true, honest answer to the question, is never hard to forget.

it's convenient to ignore how in Alaska, France, Germany, Korea, Switzerland, Belgium, Italy, Canada, Honduras, Jamaica, and Panama, or any other foreign country you visited, fought with, fought for, or trained with, and how you couldn't help but feel "equal," even superior, in their presence; and how you were treated just like another tourist, soldier, or just a man, instead of just another *"dumb ass black nigga"* but here, in your own neighborhood / city / county / state . . . country, some people, places, things, circumstances, and politics give credence to the fact that white privilege; systemic racism; discrimination and forced segregation; fear of police, and their cruelty; and overall un-equality is real, alive, and well in the good old UsA, and to experience any one of them, is never hard to forget.

Convenient To Ignore . . . Hard To Forget

(Continued 1 of 5)

it's convenient to ignore white supremacists torturing, lynching, and killing black men, and putting it on video, and no one ever gets arrested because they're friends with the good old boys in law enforcement. it's convenient to ignore Ahmad Arbery, 25, from Brunswick, Georgia, who was murdered on 23 February 2020, by two white men from the quiet Satilla Shores neighborhood. the two men claimed they thought he was a burglar, but his family said that he was just out jogging. all the killers were identified, but they were not arrested, not until it was absolutely necessary; these everyday occurrences will always be hard to forget.

it's convenient to ignore policemen, while being photographed and videoed, placing his knee on George Floyd's neck for over eight and a half minutes, while four other policemen watched unaffected, until George Floyd was dead; or a policeman being photographed, or bystanders videoing the shooting of an innocent man, in the back, at point blank range, seven times, and getting off scott-free because the black district attorney said he did not charge the cop because he did not think he could get a conviction, will always be hard to forget.

it's convenient to ignore how it felt to sit in loneliness and call it solitude; to close my eyes and dream of people without faces without color; the life lessons you've learned, the places you've visited, the things you've heard, the things you've seen, or didn't see; the people you've met, the things that you've done, and the way-stations in life that you passed, stopped by, or gone through; the companions who sojourned with you, and the many that did not have the strength, will, faith, or desire to continue; but the people, places, things, and experiences that inspire you, that touch you . . . the experiences that change your life, will always be hard to forget.

Convenient To Ignore . . . Hard To Forget

(Continued 5 of 5)

it's convenient to ignore the veterans' day parades, and all the little fat guys in funny hats, who lived for the day of the parade . . . but the sense of honor, adventure, and the comradery lost with fallen comrades is never hard to forget.

it's convenient to ignore sweetie's day, sweethearts' day, valentine's day, and forgotten invitations, anniversaries, birthdays, and all the lovers you did not love or marry, but wanted to, and the lovers you hoped would love you, but didn't . . . but a heart broken, young, or old is never had to forget.

it's convenient to ignore that it is ok to try and fail; that it is ok to make mistakes, and to dream of a better dream; that it is ok to remember who you are, where you came from, and why you are here; that you can continue to hope; that there are still young brothers and sisters out there . . . tempting fate by dreaming the impossible; but most of all, you want to remember that some things that are convenient and easy to ignore, are not always hard to forget.

it convenient to ignore the fact that one can play any game well, no matter the race, creed, or color – if given the chance, to play, and given the rules with which to play by, are the things that are often convenient to ignore, but has always been . . . and will continue to be . . . hard to forget.

A POEM IS LIKE . . .

(for Yolande Cornelia "Nikki" Giovanni, Jr. (07/43- 12/9/24)

forever, it seemed, i looked/watched you on tv, in magazines, and newspapers, then books . . . *(all of them)*.

the books have always impressed me, because they were *"your"* books . . . poetry written in secret melodies, patented for your voice . . . inspirational thoughts - words, softly riding on the wings of butterflies . . . metamorphic wisdoms heralding the news of your comings and goings . . . helping children dream, and making people take notice and pay time.

but then you disappeared, like the fleeting wind, in search of unknown spaces . . . years passed, and i thought i would never actually get to *"see"* you . . . my last hope faded when on a visit to New York . . . my plane arrived 10 minutes late from Jacksonville . . . yours arrived 5 minutes early from Cincinnati . . . our passing . . . was so brief - only a look at your back as you leaped into a taxi, then speeding off into a sea of cabs . . . in New York, it was not to be.

just when i had become content, i saw you at a reading for senior citizens at the Butterfield in Cincinnati . . . on 14 December 1979 . . . i anxiously waited for your entrance *(you were late)* and i thought . . . fate is so cruel . . . she won't come . . . but when you finally arrived, i listened and drank your every word, as you told of your unexpected need to see your dentist . . . fillings and false teeth . . . i watched with pride as you made everyone smile as you treated everyone like *"family"* . . . you were the perpetual niece, daughter, and friend . . . afterwards, i thanked you for the notes of encouragement about my first two books you had sent to me . . . however, the Butterfield closed in 2004, and was sold, but the name and the memories still remain . . . and your notes have continued to inspire.

since then, as you moved from Queens College, Rutgers, and Ohio State, i read and heard rumors, criticisms, and accusations about your nightlife . . . your friends . . . of you being an alcoholic . . . a snob . . . an exploiter . . . a white nigger . . . and a bitch . . . but i also read somewhere, that there is no such thing as "*bad*" publicity . . . so, i defended you hip and thigh.

(though you didn't care, or needed no defense)

after being called a militant poet in the early days, now they say you are one of the best African American poets emerging from the 1960s black power and black arts movements; a commentator with over 28 books published; and the title of University Distinguished Professor of English at Virginia Tech University in Blacksburg, Virginia.

(now ain't that somethin'!)

i'm happy you found someone to share your life with, and i'm sorry that you suffered through cancer, but glad that you recovered . . . for just a moment.

i'm also sad that it will keep you from your bucket list dream of going into outer space someday.

i feel that i always understood why you liked to be alone . . . solitude is where one can stop being busy . . . it is where one can disconnect and recharge . . . it is also there ,one has the opportunity to re/discover ones 'self, and find their voice again . . . it is there that one can be creative and dream . . . a place where metaphors/ laughter/ friendship/ and respect are born . . .

it has always been in my moments of solitude that you have invaded my mind, and filled my thoughts with motivation and insights from your videos, and the poetry you wrote, and from those inspirational notes you sent me . . . and it is also there that remember that you once said:

"a poem is like . . . writing a letter to your very best friend."

so, i decided to write this letter to you, to thank you for being a living note of encouragement to me, and for the many others that have found their own voice . . . and for the few who are still looking.

you're gone now . . .
and my heart is broken, and my sad eyes bleed with heart felt tears because i will deeply miss you, and you won't be able to read this letter . . . from one of your very best friends.

YOU DESERVE A MEDAL

(For Mrs. Horvena E. Alexander (1922 - 2023)
(and Mrs. Rosa E. Calloway (1925 - 2012) NYC/
Counselors at Clyde V. Courter Technical HS

you both deserve a medal
for all you have done for/to
me
you went beyond the call of duty
to save me . . .
to save me from all the corrupt versions
of myself
and all the errors of my past

i had become comfortable with living
on the poor edge of nothing
living with all my verbal good intentions
that only resulted in bad execution
but really, they were just excuses

you taught me to look past my adversities
and to take responsibility for what i could control you
introduced me to possibilities and dreams
and taught me that being poor doesn't define a person
and being poor was no excuse for not being
exceptional

you taught me about trusting others
but even more . . .
you taught me about trusting myself
and about *seeing* myself
and what i really wanted to become
and at the same time
you opened my eyes and my soul
and poured in wisdom, understanding, and love
and healed the broken parts with loving smiles
warm hugs, and kind words of encouragement

You Deserve A Medal

(Continued)

you ladies . . .
were like one of those forest fires
that they talk about
scorching the earth
to only bring forth a second spring of
new life
of new hope
for everything in its path
truth and gratitude are all i can share
for what you did for me
this *"little ghetto boy"*
and all the others . . .
that no one knows about . . .

USA Retired, 1/1995
E. Gene Givens, Major, RA, U.S. Army Corps of Engineers, 1981-1995
Master's Degree in Management, FIT, 12/1993
Master's Certificate in Government Contracting, GWU, 4/1993 BSBA,
BSBA, Management, Xavier University, 8/1981 (Class of 1982)
Athenaeum Prize For Poetry, Xavier University, 4/1980
President, Xavier Afro-American Student Association 1979-1980
Yeoman 1st Class Petty Officer, U.S. Coast Guard, 1969-1979
Clyde V. Courter Technical High School, Cincinnati, OH - Class of 1969

PRINCE OF THE CITY

(EJM 1998 - 2024)

my soul is troubled, and my tears flow like a mountain stream
because the news has come that we have lost the Prince
a man that meant so much to us all

all who knew the Prince, are mourning his passing
sadden by the news that one of the Robbinsville's flocks
will soar no more

it is said that a great man does not seek to lead, he is called to it
and he answers - that was *Elijah J. McNeil* - my Prince
he was known as one of the true leaders of the flock
he was even known as "*The Don*" among his close friends
it is said that he was a superb athlete; that God had blessed him
with strength, endurance, agility, and speed
while he excelled in all the sports that he took part in

he was often considered to be a man among boys as he instilled the principles of leadership, ambition, determination, and confidence in all others around him

he also encouraged others to always stand their ground
concerning their beliefs, to seek excellence and to walk
among crowds with confidence and self-assurance

it is said that he was a faithful friend; that he was a guiding light; that he was an adventurous soul; that he was a helpful soul; that he was a happy soul; one that loved everyone

only god, and a few others, knew the inner workings of his soul
but still, he left a lifelong lasting impression on all in the community
and all who knew of him

Elijah was loved by many – family, friends, parents,
associates, admirers, and students alike
he was taken far too soon, but his legacy will live on
and he will not be forgotten, as his spirit will continue
to fly over the skies of Robbinsville, New Jersey

Elijah was only here for a moment
but he was a once in a generation individual

Elijah lit up the room with his energy, his smile, and his laughter
he will be sorely missed by his devoted and loving mother, father
sister, cousins, aunts and uncles, grandparents . . .
and his court of lifelong friends

Elijah was always the Prince of our hearts
our Prince . . .

the Prince Of The City

ON MY WAY HOME

i was young when i started my journey
on the road trying to get home
the road has been long
and the road have been rocky
as i made my way home

sometimes . . .
the road was rough
and the hills were many
i ran into a few mountains
that i had started to climb
but each mountain
was higher than i thought
and things had grown very, very, dark
trying to get home

i had gotten tired and weary on my journey
trying to find my way home
even though i cried, stumbled, and fell many times
i never lost my spirit, my faith, and my determination
in my efforts to get home

on my way home
i ran into some good people
that felt just like family
but i also ran into some mean and evil spirited people . . .
people that did not mean me well
and my path led me to several places
that often seemed like a living hell
and when i thought times were too hard
i knelt and prayed
in the old-time way

On My Way Home

(Continued)

i asked my savior to give me strength . . .
strength to go around and through those obstacles
that were in my way

he answered all my prayers
and i thanked him
for his protection
and his love, favor, and grace
while he guided me on my way

he renewed my strength so i could travel
along those long, rough, steep, and rocky roads
and to climb those hills and mountain
day by day

he gave me a path to deal with those
mean-spirited people
in a kind and gentle way

on my long way home
i became a better man
and learned that it is the journey
not the destination
that makes a man appreciate
who they really are

now i smile, and give thanks for his favor
and pray for those along my way
as i try to stay centered
keeping the main thing the main thing
and always look for the blessings, in every day
as i travel on this long, perilous journey
trying to find my way home
as my savior lights my way

www.ingramcontent.com/pod-product-compliance
Lightning Source LLC
Chambersburg PA
CBHW022115050726
47591CB00002B/792

* 9 7 8 1 9 6 9 3 6 7 8 7 8 *